101 FUN FAMILY ACTIVITIES

THE SELF-ISOLATION SURVIVAL GUIDE

By Laureen Kuhl

101 Fun Family Activities, The Self Isolation Survival Guide
by Laureen Kuhl

First Published by Possibility Press

Graphics and editing by Maureen Reese

Kuhl, Laureen
    101 Fun Family Activities The Self Isolation Survival Guide/ Laureen Kuhl
p. cm.
Includes Index
ISBN:978-0-9866716-3-0

For my family,
with much love.

Without you, this never would have been created.

INDEX

1

. . . .

We've all been there. It's late. The rest of the family is asleep, but you're clinging on to precious "me" time, barely watching your phone through drooping eyelids, your fingers locked on permanent scroll, videos streaming past at the speed of light. An ad bursts through your haze.

"Do you wish for a better life?"

Oh yeah, absolutely. Who doesn't?!

You click through to the site and see something like this…

"I used to be just like you, overworked, under paid, with a boss who demanded more hours from my already exhausted week. My family barely remembered who I was. Now, I'm living the dream of working remotely. I work from home, enjoying play time with my family, here on the beaches of Aruba. I have it all, money, time, family, and you can too!"

With a sales pitch like that, they could sell anything! After all, they're selling a dream, a dream everyone wants to buy.

I want to go to Aruba!

I like easy money!

I'd love leisure time with my family!

Until recently tying that dream to working remotely probably paid out big time for… whoever was selling. Since the virus has forced everyone to work from home, people are discovering that actually being at home 24-7 is a little less dream, and a little more challenging reality. Being forced to live out the dream, as you must during an isolation order can turn that challenging reality into a nightmare. But it doesn't have to be that way. There are ways to not only manage the enforced time together, but to thrive in difficult circumstances.

Cut to fourteen years ago. I was raising four kids under the age of four in northern Ontario where it was the norm to endure three months of -30 weather. I was in the midst of a deep, difficult isolation. The kids were full of curiosity, energy, and demands for my attention. I usually saw my husband for only a few hours a day, and sometimes he was away for weeks at a time. I rarely saw, or talked to, anyone else in person. Even though I am a bit of an introvert the isolation was taking a tole on my sanity. I needed to get out of the house. I needed to breathe the free air. I needed to talk to someone about something other than cartoon characters and dirty diapers.

But it wasn't really possible for me to break the isolation. Taking four small children out of the house on my own was difficult at the best of times. In the middle of winter it was impossible.

Not only would I have to make sure that each child was swaddled in the correct number of snowsuits, I had to ensure they wouldn't take anything off until we reached our destination! Ask anyone who has lived that far north… you don't play chicken with -30. Needless to say, I didn't leave the house unless it was absolutely necessary.

Those were long difficult days. There were some weeks when we didn't get out at all! I stopped changing out of my pyjamas. What was the point? I wasn't going anywhere and no one was coming to visit. Nights turned into days, days turned into weeks, weeks turned into months. My pyjamas felt more like smelly prison gear, and less like a luxurious leisure suit. I lost track of time. The lack of structure and routine that was so appealing on day one, felt like a crushing avalanche of surprise moments. I couldn't cope with all the needs, emotions and challenges that came at me on a moment to moment basis. It seemed as though we were alone on an island and I would never see another human being again! I had careened to the brink of what I could manage and was wondering if I would ever find my way back to normal.

Thankfully that wasn't the end of my story.

It took a lot of trial and error, careful thought and planning to figure out how to manage the isolation, but it was time well spent, because those three months of isolation happened every year! In the end, we managed to get through the isolation, sanity intact, and even enjoyed our time together. Yes, our time in isolation was very challenging, but it also presented us with good days, creative opportunities and many memorable moments.

Necessity is the mother of invention and I had to be very inventive to keep my kids from climbing the walls or myself from screaming into my pillow.

I have compiled a list of things that worked for me over the years. I hope they inspire you as much as they inspired us. It may be tempting to skip straight to the activities chapter and if you are desperate, by all means, skip away, (Chapter 4 - 101 Things to Do In Isolation, pg.19. And you're welcome for not making you figure it out on your own) but if you have a few seconds of patience left in your isolation tank please take a moment to read through the other chapters. While learning to manage the isolation is certainly not as exciting, it will make all the difference to your day to day life and benefit your entire family. It's my hope that the hard won

lessons I learned in deep isolation will spread a little hope
and joy into your lives during this time. Isolation with the family can be very challenging, but…

take courage my friends,
it will all be ok.

2

Oh, how much I wish I was Maria. You know the one. Maria. "Sound of Music" Maria. Yep. Of course. The Classic Perfect Parent. Her kids sat happily at her feet as she taught them the basics of music. Her kids followed her through town like the pied piper. Her kids hid quietly while the Nazis searched the graveyard. Could we manage that? Even if our lives depended on it, I'm not sure. Depends if the kids are within holding distance. And did you see that puppet show? How did she get the kids to sit still long enough to paint the puppets, let alone co-operate for a whole show? I say this as someone who actually puts together shows and directs large casts for a living… are you kidding?

Perfect? Please. I would settle for walking somewhere without losing a child.

Regular family life is challenging, but life in isolation is a far cry from any idyllic film. If you're isolated with toddlers you will soon be longing for that Aruba beach, an attentive nanny, and unlimited massages. You can forget singing songs! Survival is everything! But it doesn't have to be that way.

Finding the balance between what you hope for and what you can manage is a constant struggle, but it is a struggle well worth the effort.

In order to manage the isolation, I recommend a few ground rules:

Be kind to yourself.

Forgive your mistakes.

Forgive your spouse's mistakes.

Forgive your child's mistakes.

Look for the little things that bring you joy.

Your life isn't a movie. It's real life.

Real life is good, but messy.

You don't have to impress someone.

You need to be present.

You need to establish a routine.

You need to keep trying.

You don't have to be perfect.

That list that took a lot of hard lessons to make. The last item on the list in particular is a big one, especially coming from me, a recovering perfectionist!

Frankly, life in isolation is far from perfect, but do your best to be present in the moment as much as possible and persistent in your goal to create a good life for yourself and for those for whom you care. Carefully laid out plans will fail. Unimagined crisis will happen. Some days you'll be lucky to get out of your pyjamas before it's time to hit the pillow. That's ok. As my husband once told me "If you're ok, and the kids are ok, you can consider that a successful day."

You may be able to manage whole groups of adults, see great, difficult projects through to the finish line, and have a shelf full of manager of the year trophies, but children and isolation have a way of reducing your skills to a smouldering ash heap.

It's a whole new level of difficulty, that's all.

I was once told that looking after children is like herding cats. Think about it. It's got to be pretty close. Just when you've got them moving in one direction, they take off in another. They don't want to be herded. They want to be free! It's easy to despair when plans fail, but it's all ok. And it doesn't mean you should give up on having a plan.

A decent plan, and a goal you believe in will keep you going when disaster strikes. There's always tomorrow. Pick yourself up, brush yourself off, and start all over again.

Set a routine and stick to it.

Set a daily routine. Set a weekly routine. Make the weekend a little different from the weekdays. Keep your family's current routine in mind when you set the new one so that it isn't too difficult to manage the transition.

Why is this important? A routine will not only help you remember what day it is, it will make you feel like you've accomplished something on a daily basis, even if that something was getting out of bed and eating breakfast.

A good routine will make everyone feel productive. One of the worst things about isolation is the sense of helpless waiting that can make you despair. Getting up, getting dressed, doing something on a regular basis will not only help the time pass, it will give you a little bit of control over your situation. Believe me, you'll need it, and you can do it!

The necessity of creating a routine was a particularly hard won truth for me. I'm an artist who loves to try new things. No one can tell me what to do! No one can tie me down! My freedom is essential to who I am!

I remember crying over the first schedule I ever made. And not just crying, full on, throw myself on my pillow, drama tears. Farewell sense of adventure! I'm going to be hemmed in, held down and my creative life is over! You can't tell I am a theatre kid, can you? Absolutely no drama. But seriously, routines and schedules are vital. They give you the momentum to get things done, even when you are sure you can't keep going. They make sure that you have time for things and people you consider important. They allow you to reach goals. Routines have been key to my artistic success. And they are especially important when you are trying to work from home, or when you can't leave your home for a long time.

Making a manageable work/life routine will enable you to get work done on time. It will help you estimate how much time and effort is left in a project, which can be key if a boss or client is depending on you to finish a task. A routine will also allow you to have some quiet work time, or frankly, rest time while your children are awake…when the kids are little this is a challenge you can't ignore! So set a routine, stick to the routine, and if you get off the routine, be brave and find a way back to it! It's worth it.

There are more reasons to develop a routine. When you are an isolated parent you aren't looking at a day full of quality time where your child has your full and undivided attention for as long as you are with them, you would never be alone! You would be exhausted by all the "fun!" Instead, you are looking at a day full of quantity time, with long stretches of togetherness where you will interact with your children in a meaningful way, from time to time.

You need to set the parameters of how much attention they will receive, and when and where they will receive it or believe me, your child will set the parameters for you. Of course, the parameters can't be unreasonable. A ten year old can manage hours alone, and can follow a routine without much guidance, while a toddler needs constant supervision from an adult.

If you have small children and you also need to work, its best that you discuss your routine with a partner or that you schedule your work time in short bursts around your child's routine. You never know what new, life threatening idea will pop into your toddler's little mind!

It's a good idea to plan to complete difficult, thoughtful tasks during the times the kids are asleep or in quiet time, but you can usually juggle some work time during the day while your child is playing. Just be aware that if you are supervising the kids, you won't have long uninterrupted moments to think or be able to complete difficult tasks. Taking care of kids is a job too, and not paying attention to that job will have any number of consequences.

Understanding your situation, how much help you have and when, and how much you can get done in the time you have, not only helps you to create a good routine, it will reduce your stress.

When you are isolated, routines become a vital lifeline. When you work outside the home, that work provides the routine and it's easy to think of home as the place where no rules apply. The vacation zone. That's fine in small doses, but to live and work from home every day without routines can be disastrous, especially with children.

Routines give children a sense of stability. They'll know what's coming and when, and to your great relief it will provide the answer to the following persistent questions:

When's supper?

When will you pay attention to me?

When is it my turn?

Do I have to go to bed?

Do I have to take a bath?

Do I have to learn stuff?

Do I have to sleep in my own bed?

For older children, routines can help them learn new skills and stay focused on their schoolwork. Routines supply structure for food, sleep, play time, and most importantly, routines tell children when they can expect your full attention and when they have to wait.

When setting your routine also remember that your child should always have full access to you when they need you. Sometimes the routine will bend because of someone's needs. Sometimes it will break. But return to the routine as soon as possible. Remember, every moment isn't an emergency, your children need routine as much as you do, and you will need breathing room if you are going to survive full time isolation.

If you are willing to take the time to add daily or weekly chores to the routine, they will provide children with a set of responsibilities that will make them feel important and valued.

We all struggle with being unable to *do* something about our isolation. Routines and responsibilities help all of us regain some sense of order and control. Even little kids can do a simple chore like helping to find their clothes, learning to fold, or being the person who is responsible for closing the cupboard when your hands are full. Big kids can be responsible for their own cleaning and cleaning the house in general. They can also learn to cook. Yes, your food may taste funny for a while. Yes, your bathroom may lack…refinement.Yes, they will complain a lot while you establish the routine of chores, and frankly you'll be tired of telling them what to do and fixing their mistakes, but stick to it! You'll be surprised by how much your kids are able to do, how much consistent practice causes them to improve and by what tasks are willing to take on.

Be aware, you'll need at least one consistent week to establish any new routine. You might need more. It depends on the kid and it depends on what you've expected in the past.

Remind yourself of the routine's importance. Imagine how great it will be for them to master the new skills. Do your best to be patient with them and with yourself. You may have to change the routine to fit what you and your children can handle, and/or you might spend a large part of the week corralling the troops back to the routine trail. Don't lose heart. It will be worth your trouble.

3

. . . .

Once you've established a good routine, be willing to be flexible with the routine. Everyone needs some downtime and we all need to blow off steam. It's a really good idea to create a "relaxing weekend" break from the every day routine. You'll need it, the kids need it, and everyone will enjoy the break from the ordinary. Give the whole family a pyjama day (or two), have a mini movie marathon, eat everyone's favourite snack, or take an idea off my list, the choice is yours!

You see, while I'm not talking about the dream of working from your Aruba beach office while the children play on the sand, I *am* talking about how to balance your life, while managing more togetherness than you ever intended!

If your children are older, you might have long stretches of uninterrupted quiet but very little cleaning, lots of hormones and pent up energy. If the kids are little, they have the potential to exhaust you with endless cries for attention, or to wear out your patience while you constantly leap into action to save their lives! You may not have the dream life you thought you'd have, but you can have a good life. You can have a moment or two on your own, you can have time after they go to bed for naps and/or nighttime, you will be able to quietly make supper (not *all* the time, but at least some of the time!), and you can reduce the number of times your kids climb all over you and won't leave you alone.

These seem like ridiculously small goals, but in isolation, that's where you are, in a world of small goals.

Family Activities

These "special events" are fun for kids of all ages, but they work particularly well with toddlers to 10 year olds. You'll be pleasantly surprised at how engaging these tasks can be... and how much time they can fill!

I highly recommend these events as *a break from the ordinary routine*, not as an every day affair. Kids and adults alike can enjoy these breaks from the ordinary, but to attempt to do this everyday would be to lose the "specialness" of the event. What would normally be an entertaining and exciting break will turn into an exhausting exercise for everyone involved. So, be kind to yourself. Relax. You aren't a contestant in a parent of the year tournament, you're just trying to enjoy your time together.

As parents, it's difficult to allow your kids to participate in the creation of the event. I know I often have a vision for how the event *should* go and being creative, I can easily take over the whole process. Remember, you may know how amazing *your* event throwing skills are, but your children will appreciate being centrally involved in the event, and to your relief, the preparation will engage their time and attention. In other words, let them participate. You'll get a break. The event may not be up to the standards of a fully adult production, but if you allow kids to create, you'll be pleased by their excitement, and you'll enjoy the result. It's less about the product and more about the process. The kids will love the attention they get from creating this wonderful event, and you'll love that they won't be driving you crazy!

The ideas that follow are only really meant as inspiration. Remember, nothing beats listening to your child for wonderful new ideas, and nothing trumps understanding your needs and boundaries as a parent. Once you've tried a few don't be surprised if your whole family starts making up new ideas, it really is addicting!

4

1. **Make an extended blanket fort.** Drape blankets over tables and chairs, put pillows on the floor and cuddle up inside. Kids enjoy taking their toys and books inside, crawling in and out of the various "doorways" and creating new rooms. Parents enjoy the muffled silence.

2. **Create a zoo.** Have the kids collect all the stuffed animals and create zones for the creatures. The Savana, The Arctic Circle, The Ocean. Encourage them to make signs and even come up with a zoo keeper costume of their choice. Give them a time limit (sometimes you can stretch this to all day) and tell them that they will be in charge of giving you a zoo tour at that time. If you want to get all educational in their business, help them look up some facts about the animals in their care. Encourage them to learn it for the tour. They could write it on a clipboard or record it ahead and play it during the tour if they are shy. Have them make up zoo themed names for their snacks and meals. It's pretty fun to see how creative they get with this one. Note* If your child wants to do a "water" or "sand" zone… beware! My creative children put their stuffed animals in the tub and almost soaked them before I realized what they were doing.

3. **Monk's Dinner.** This is perfect for an "I'd do anything for some silence" day. Have everyone wear their "robe" (bathrobe will do) and come to dinner silently. Set the rules: Everyone has taken a "vow of silence." All dinner interactions must be conferred silently. If someone "breaks their vow" you choose the consequences. Depending on age they can, lose a utensil, have more vegetables added to their plate, or, if you've been timing how long the family can be silent, the timer gets reset. Competition will ensue. This is a great if everyone has been a little too loud and it's a sneaky way to get a little silence into your day.

4. **Finger Painting, the Safe Way.** Put the kids in their bathing suits and plop them in the tub with some paper and washable paint. I was fond of finger paint but anything that washes off easily is more than acceptable. Let them paint. When everyone has completed their masterpiece, remove the painting and rinse off the kiddies. You're happy because you have less to clean, they're happy because the rinsed off paint makes "rainbow trails" all the way to the drain. Win, win.

5. **River Boating.** Here's another idea for calming kids down and inducing some silence. Play some relaxing, quiet music, I highly recommend classical pieces like Delibes "Lakmé," or Beethoven's "Moonlight Sonata," but really anything soothing will do. If the children are small enough, have them sit on a blanket, tablecloth or sheet and pull them across the floor. If they are too big have

them make "boats" by decorating a box. They can then slide around after you, their "Gondolier," as you "float" on the water. Make trips around the room and have them tell you (in a whisper) what sites they "see"... a castle? ... a forest? ... the moon? When they start to get bored have them rearrange the room to "change the sights." Put stuffed animals in different areas to "surprise" you or their sibling. Have them find pictures in books or draw a picture and place it around the area.Have one of the kids dress up and wave from the "shore." Offer to take turns riding or pulling with the kids. While this activity won't take long, it was a favourite for my kids and provided some quiet for me.

6. **Indoor sandbox.** Lay down a tablecloth, pour cornmeal or rice into a deep cooking pan. Give the kids a variety of safe utensils to dig and pour to their hearts content. This is a great way to keep little kids entertained in the kitchen while you make dinner. Note* Even with the tablecloth, this is a potential mess maker, and little kids may be tempted to eat the "sand." I highly recommend using edible, safe "sand" and watching the kids closely with this one.

7. **Drive In Movie Theatre.** If you have access to large cardboard boxes, or are willing to use your clothes hamper, you have all the makings of a super car! The children can decorate a box per child as their own personal dream machine. Or lay out towels on the ground to indicate the parameters of the "car"and let them make it comfy with pillows and blankets. Choose a movie or show as a fami-

ly. Have them "order" movie snacks from a list of available food. They can either make a little drive in concession stand, or you can deliver their snacks to their "car." Watch the show together.

8. **Make a movie.** Have the kids create a story or choose a story from one of their favourite books. Encourage them to find costumes, create a story board (pictures of what scenes they want in the movie, and the order the scenes need to go in) and "build" a set. When they are ready and have rehearsed, record them on your camera or phone. For older kids, this one get very complicated and can take all day.

9. **Beach Day.** Lay out towels. Put on some beach wear. Play summer music, like the Beach Boys, Bangles, Bananarama or chose a summer streaming list. Read books. If you have enough space you can play beach ball or frisbee. Look up summer drinks on the internet and make a pitcher, have summer snacks and food. Let the kids play in the tub or shower in their swimsuits. Watch videos of the ocean, or check out underwater animals in picture books, online or in animal documentaries. This is a great one for those winter blahs.

10. **Olympics day.** Have the children find and collect "gym equipment" from around the house. If you don't have gym equipment, you can pull a mattress off a bed for tumbling, pile books to jump over, lay out cans and cereal boxes to make an obstacle course, use cans as weights for a

"weight lifting contest." Have the kids make a score board and a trophy. Once everything is assembled play some triumphant music and have the "contestants" parade in. Have everyone perform the events. Play music for the awards ceremony. Use your phone to time the contestants and be sure to video/take photos!

11. **Stations.** You've seen this technique at work in your kid's kindergarten class, but stations work well for any age. Have the kids help you set up games, crafts, books, snacks or really any thing you all enjoy, at different tables or even in different rooms. Assign at least two people to a station. Set a timer. When the timer goes off rotate to another table. You can rotate all together or get creative by dividing the group in two and rotating in different directions. For young children set the timer fairly short, but for older kids you can set the timer at 20 minutes or higher.

12. **Indoor Picnic.** Spread a tablecloth on the floor or bring in a small picnic table. Use paper plates and cups. If you have a picnic basket, great, use it too. Have the kids help "make" the picnic and put it into the basket, or backpacks. It's your choice if you want them to take the picnic with them during this next part, use your best judgement. Have them go on a "hike" through the house, journalling what they see either by drawing a picture, writing in a journal or taking a photo. Have everyone join you for the picnic and ask each person to talk about their journey. You can even incorporate a nap or quiet time into the event by telling them to find a quiet place for a rest.

13. **Box tunnel/house/village.** Find several cardboard boxes of different sizes. Build a tunnel, house or village by opening both ends of the boxes and sticking them to-gether using strong tape. Packing tape or duct tape work well, glue and masking tape not so much. Cut out win-dows and doors, but don't let your ingenuity stop there... why not make elevators, pulley systems and car race-tracks? You can colour the boxes any way you want. Chose your location for assembly wisely. Making some-thing this large is a lot of fun and the result is often used for several days, if not weeks, after you create it. Either assemble it in pieces that can be easily taken apart and put back together, or assemble it somewhere that it won't bug you to work around. My brother and I used to make these on a semi-regular basis and I remember begging my mom to let us do everything in our little house, watch TV, eat, sleep. Once our house was no longer, Ahem, stable, it would mysteriously disappear and we would long for the next big package to arrive so we could start again. My mother was no fool!

14. **Travel without Traveling.** Go through your streaming account or video collection and look for documentaries on a place you would like to go. Get the family to research food, outfits, useful phrases etc. Don't make it too difficult for yourself, this is less an exercise in perfection and more a fun way to pass time and enjoy life together. Get dressed in travelling outfits, make a local meal and watch the documentary as you eat.

15. **Miniputt course.** This won't work for everyone, especially if you have hard hitting, enthusiastic children! Use your own judgement. Make a golf course in your house using any room you feel is "safe enough." Make holes and set up obstacles. You can snake towels on the floor for "rough," use pillows as sand pits. Get creative on the holes. You can use jars, toilet paper rolls, cardboard boxes, gift bags… sky's the limit. As long as the ball has a place to go in you're good to go! Have the kids create a sign for your course, hole numbers, and score cards. Perhaps one of them would like to run the drink and snack cart or prefers to caddy? That's fine. You don't have a club? Well, you've just upped the level of difficulty! Kitchen utensils will work just fine as long as everyone has a "club" that is relatively similar in size and shape, you may just have to bend a lot lower to the ball, that's all. If your family enjoys this, you can certainly keep some of the course and rearrange it for another time.

16. **Cooking Show.** Get the kids to help with supper. If you want the experience to last a good part of the day get them to research the food and make a menu, title and select music. One kid or adult is the "filmmaker" videoing the experience for everyone. Dig out aprons or create DIY versions by pinning a tea towels to your shirt and tying a belt around your middle. Little kids can help with things like mixing the salad or setting the table or selecting the music, while big kids can help with everything else. Have the filmmaker get the "stars" to describe in detail everything that they are doing. "Fancy voices" are en-

couraged. Keep the movie short and fun. When supper is done go watch your own cooking show together.

17. **Make a mural.** Unfold a large box, use a big sheet of paper or if you don't have a big sheet of paper, tape together many sheets as you like and use the "untaped" side for your picture. As a group decide on the theme of the mural. Are you recreating a special location? A beach? A cafe? A sunset? Or are you creating something from your imagination? Have everyone choose something to focus on. Perhaps you're recreating a cafe. One person is in charge of drawing chairs and tables, another in charge of drawing customers, another in charge of drawing food. Or maybe someone likes to draw and someone else likes to colour. That's ok too. It works best if everyone works together as a team but it's also possible for each person to decorate their own area of the mural. Use your best judgement. I found this one works best in small doses over several days. Once people start losing interest fold it up and bring it out again another time. After a while this group project will take on a life of its own!

18. **Indoor scavenger hunt.** Make a list of items people are likely to find in the house. Depending on the age of the kids, make the list long and difficult or easy and short. If you're really feeling clever this game can be turned into a cleanup routine. Instead of asking the children to bring you an item to collect points, the points are collected when the item is found and put away in its proper spot. ie: Find and put away 3 pointy toys, 6 matching socks, 4 shoes etc.

19. **Lava world.** This one does take a little planning but it can be a lot of fun and will wear off some pent up energy. Pick a spot in the house to start from and a finish line. Using rugs, chairs, couches, pillows etc., you must travel to the finish line without touching the floor with any part of your body. You can have "safe zones," "designated lava heroes" (adults who are immune to lava for helping little guys), and "lava flows" where the lava level gets higher than the floor. The first person to the finish line wins.

20. **Lava world 2.0.** No finish line. The last person standing rules the world!

21. **Fancy Dinner Out.** Candles, romantic music, stunning views, what could be better? Have the kids create a restaurant. It's up to you if you'd like them to actually make the food, but frankly this is less about what you're eating, and more about the experience of eating in a restaurant. Have the kids make up a menu and set the table. If they can find pictures of stunning views to be the "windows" of the restaurant, even better. Have your children be the waiters, get them to collect everyone's order and relay it to the kitchen. Set a time for the meal. Have everyone get dressed up in their fancy clothes and "meet" at the entrance. Let the waiters seat you. Serve the meal with low lighting and candles ...Hint: the low lighting really helps quiet everyone down! Pretend to pay the bill and make sure everyone helps clean up!

22. **Hide and seek.** This is a favourite of little guys and can be a particularly funny experience for adults. There's nothing like pretending you can't see your toddler hiding behind a floor lamp. For slightly older kids be sure to give off limits to dangerous areas like chests, appliances or workshops. They will be inventive and safety first!

23. **Sardines.** Reverse hide and seek. One person hides, everyone goes to look for that person. If someone manages to find the hider, they squeeze into the hiding space with them. The game ends when the last seeker finds the hider. Then start all over again with the last finder becoming the hider. This game quickly becomes hilarious. Trying to squeeze five people in a closet is very entertaining.

24. **Sock puppet show.** Go through your mismatched socks box, come on, we all have one, and select some loners. Make puppets by sewing or glueing on buttons, or using stickers for eyes. If you are extra creative you can make costumes and sew faces on the socks. Either create a little puppet theatre from cardboard boxes or just have the kids duck behind the couch to present their puppet show. Depending on the age of the kids you can get them to write out the show or recreate scenes from their favourite book or movie.

25. **Library.** Another "quiet" event. Have the kids bring books into one room in the house. Bring in comfy chairs, play relaxing music, turn the lights down low and either have reading lamps or let the kids have a flashlight. Once everything is set up, take everyone out of the room and

declare "we're going to the library!" It works well to give them a time frame. "We're going to be there for one hour." Let them know that it's very important for everyone to be quiet at the library or the librarian will get you in trouble. Everyone enters the "library" and reads or plays quietly. This works particularly well for those kids who need a nap, but no longer take one. It is, essentially, quiet time with a fancy name. Just don't let them know!

26. **Store.** If you're really clever this can be an inventive way to get the kids to reorganize their toys or your pantry cupboard and learn to add. Have them make a sign for their store and if you have fake money now is the time to pull it out. You could also have them make pretend credit cards, but it does make adding a little more tricky. The kids arrange the store displays and either price them or decide on a price later. Take turns being the sales person or the customer. They can either use a calculator or add, but it is always fun to push buttons and open drawers so use a box or a small cupboard as the cash register station. Have the cashier load the customer's goods in a bag and say "Thanks for shopping!"

27. **Dance party!** Clear the floor, put on the tunes and wiggle to the beat. You can also turn down the lights and use flash lights to create a "light show. " A dance party is also a good excuse to try out all your kid's glow in the dark clothes!

28. **Science experiments.** It's a good idea to do this as a group, one experiment at a time. There are so many resources online for engaging experiments, many of which are as exciting as watching a magic trick. Potato batteries and Lava mountains are particular favourites, but filling the bathtub or sink and testing what floats is also a sure hit. If your family enjoys this (and you have the time) it would be worth considering setting one up once a week, and letting the kids research for experiments they want to try next.

29. **Make play dough or slime.** While this does require your supervision the ingredients are simple and easy to get, and the extra playtime mileage is worth the effort. There are so many good recipes out there and while the making is painless, the kids will enjoy lots of playtime with it afterwards, especially since they helped make it! Note: make some rules as to where they play with this! As someone who has removed both of these items from carpet and clothes it is a hassle to clean! Have them use a placemat and designate a slime/dough playing area. You can thank me later.

30. **Create a race track and have a race.** You can do this many different ways. If you already have cars it is certainly easier, but you can create your own "car" out of anything that rolls. Creating the track is just as much fun. Build a track with lego. Make a "track" on the floor by lining the borders with soup cans. Cut and glue cardboard boxes together to make a ramp. I've even seen one genius track that was built entirely out of toilet paper rolls! The track was hung on a door and the car, inserted at the

top, zipped and flipped the whole way down to the bottom. It did look like fun! This easily becomes educational by making the kids test which "car" goes the fastest and why, what surface for the track works best and perform experiments on increasing stability in their vehicle or track.

31. **Make an art gallery.** Have the kids create pictures, sculptures, "mixed media," or pull from their "repertoire." Designate a gallery space. Set the art up. Use books to make a stand for sculptures, take down a couple a of pictures that are already hanging on your walls and tie a string between the nails, use clothes pins, hair clips or safety pins to hang the art from the string. Write up a description for their art work or have the kids write one of their own. To make it a little more "professional" use a template like this:

Artist Name (b.birthdate)
Name of Artist's Work, date created
What materials they used to create the art
Description of art and what it means to them.

When everyone has finished making the art, have them go out of the room and come back in as the "guests of the art gallery" during the grand opening. Take photos. Send video footage to the grandparents. Have each person describe their art in detail. Hopefully they'll let you take it down at some point.

32. **Read a long book.** Select one of your favourite books or one that the kids are interested in, but is just above their reading level. Set pillows on the floor and read them one chapter a week, or as much as they can sit for at a time. When my kids were little I read "The Hobbit" to them, because apparently I like to aim high… and really I just wanted to read it and had so little time! It was an effort at first, but before long my littlest kids were asking me to read more from "the story of the one old guy and the other old guy." I'm still not sure how much they remember of the actual book, but they enjoyed the routine and the attention and I enjoyed reading. Win, win.

33. **Marble Maze.** Depending on the age and interest of the children the maze can either be created "large sized" using cereal boxes, books and paper tubes on your floor, or "small sized" by cutting and gluing together bits of cardboard, card stock or wood to a hard, non-bendy surface, like thick cardboard or wood. Once you've created your maze try to weave your marble through the maze. You can use a larger ball for the larger maze if you wish.

34. **Costume Party.** For some kids, every day is a costume party, but you can make this special by designating a time, place and snacks for the party. Have the kids make and deliver invitations. Take photos and videos. Have a fashion show. The options are endless.

35. **Make video messages or online cards for loved ones.** We all know the grandparents would like to hear from their grandkids more often, but it can be hard to get the

kids to talk for long and even harder to set aside time for the call to happen. Video your child describing a favourite toy. Have them choose a nice card. Send the whole project to your loved ones and enjoy the accolades.

36. **Family Talent Show.** Kids always want to show you something, this is just a way to collect all those some-things into one place and time. Have your kids practice their talent, paint their painting, write their story and give them a time and place for their performance. When the time comes, have your friends or relatives video call in (maybe they would like to share their talents too?) Set up chairs. Dim the lights. Announce each child and their talent. Clap loudly and enjoy!

37. **Kid friendly/adult friendly podcasts.** There are few story tellers who fit in the zone of fun to listen to for kids and enjoyable for adults. Gather the family in one room. Set pillows on the floor for comfort. Get snacks. Let them cuddle in blankets. Turn down the lights. Download, stream or... old school play some podcasts on your speaker. Some entertainers we've enjoyed include: Stewart MacLean (I highly recommend "Dave Toilet Trains the Cat,") Garrison Keillor, and Robert Munsch.

38. **Tea party.** Set up your kitchen table with "tea" (juice for little guys) in a tea pot, and cookies. Use special glasses, or tea cups if you have them. Have your child "invite" their favourite dolls and stuffed animals and encourage them to "dress fancy" for the occasion. Stream classical music. Ask questions like "How are you enjoying this lovely

weather?", "Is it a good idea to wear black before labour day?" And "Do you think the stock market will recover?" Really the more "grown up" the question, the more fun it is to hear your kid tackle it. The answers can be hilarious.

39. **Traditional Dance around the world.** Find a traditional dance on Youtube. Attempt to learn it as a family. Record your fancy moves! Stun crowds at the next wedding. You know you want to!

40. **Ask Siri or Alexa silly questions and see how she responds!** This works particularly well to distract the child while you have to wait for something.

41. **Newscast.** Make up fake news stories or have the kids choose moments from their day. Make the news as dramatic as possible. Kid courts disaster by eating breakfast cereal with a fork. Dad starts fire, cooks dinner. Live footage of the bird feeder thief! Have the kids choose or make a news desk, their reporter costumes and film the news. Older kids can even edit this together and insert footage!

42. **The Seven Wonders of the World.** Have the kids research the seven wonders of the world, modern or ancient it doesn't matter. Have them create something with the info. Choose a wonder and draw it, create a model. Write or make up a report on what they've learned and especially how they think this wonder came to be. After all, the wonders are some of the great mysteries of

mankind, no one really knows how they were made! Pick a time when they'll present their findings to everyone. Watch and learn.

43. **Sugar cookies.** Fun to make, fun to cut out shapes, fun to decorate, and fun to eat, these cookies are a labour of love but also provide many engaging moments. Plan to space the cookie making out, even over a couple of days. The dough has to be refrigerated in order to cut the cookies and the cookies need to rest after baking in order to decorate them so it's less stressful to spread the whole event out, even if waiting can be challenging.

44. **Colouring contest.** This can be as serious or as casual a contest as you wish. Everyone should participate and you can display your drawings afterwards. It's up to you if you want everyone to "judge" the pictures and declare a winner, but it can be fun to see what people create.

45. **Portraits.** Draw portraits of each other, or have the kids look in the mirror and draw portraits of themselves. You can also up the difficulty level by having the kids look at the side profile shadow of a sibling and draw their silhouette! Take the portraits and hang them on each person's bedroom door, or send in the mail to loved ones.

46. **Movie marathon.** Decide on a movie or series. Plan this as an "event" for the end of the week so that the excitement builds! Have snacks and marathon away.

47. **Puzzle.** Pull down some tricky puzzles from your shelf. Choose a reasonable sized puzzle and set up out of the way. Work away at it together from time to time. It's good to see a long term project come together with a group effort.

48. **Call the relatives.** Make a list of your relatives and have the kids give them a call. If they are shy, you can always make a list of questions the kids can ask their relatives, and remind of them of a few key activities that they've enjoyed over the past few days.

49. **Write a letter to a penpal, relative or friend.** It can be interesting for kids to do this, it's not often that we mail letters these days. Hand written is nice, and including a picture is always a good idea, but be mindful of size and weight restrictions.

50. **Make music.** Have the kids learn an instrument, or learn to sing a song. If they are particularly into it, get them to write their own song, even if it's a short one! If they enjoy making music they will learn best if "lesson time" is built into your routine. Encourage them to keep trying, it's hard to learn this skill but very worthwhile in the end.

51. **Circus!** Collect the stuffed animals. Find some circus music. Create some costumes. Practice the acts. You can have tumbling acts, clowns, magicians, "animal" trainers, comedians, a "flea" circus (with invisible performers), and of course an announcer live from the centre ring. Have

everyone gather for the performance. You can even Zoom in the relatives.

52. **Spa Day.** Find some spa music. Have everyone wear their pyjamas and house coats. Fill the bath tub with a couple of inches of warm water. Pour in some salt. Have everyone soak their toes. Dry off and rub with cream. Apply a facial, for little guys, it might just be some cream. Cut a cucumber and have everyone lay down on towels with the cucumber over their eyes. Relax. If the kids are older and really into it you can pull out what ever else you have at home, nail polish, manicures, pedicures, hair masks, you name it. Finish with a nice hot drink and make sure to tell each other "I've never been so relaxed," and "why did we wait so long to try this!"

53. **Family Reading Competition.** See how many stories you can each read during a given time limit, a week, a day, an hour! No cheating! You can give out prizes or just the honour of being the "House Champion."

54. **DIY Pizza.** Because you can prepare pizza cold this is a great meal for little kids to pitch in. Make your own dough, or use flat bread or pita bread as a base. Canned tomato sauce works just fine, but if you're feeling fancy you can make your own. Preset your toppings so little hands can help without the danger of being around the cutting board. Shredded cheese, pepperoni and diced bell peppers are usually winners but you'll know your family's food preferences better than I do. Once the pizza is as-

sembled, pop into oven to cook/melt. At dinner have everyone admire what you made together.

55. **Super Hero Dinner.** Make your own super heroes. Perhaps you already have a costume, perhaps you don't, but I think its fun to make up brand new super heroes complete with logos like Tide-Al, Laundry Man or Wig Woman, Mistress of Halloween. Wear your costumes to dinner and ask for items using super hero voices. Say things like "Stop! What you're doing is an in-salt to that pasta!" And "Quickly! Pass me the butter before all is lost!" The kids may not want the fun to end and you can encourage them to wear their costumes and create their own hero movie…tomorrow.

56. **Flash light Tag.** Make sure you clear the area of things you could fall over. Turn out the lights. One person uses a flashlight to "tag" everyone else. Once everyone has been tagged, hand the flashlight to someone else and start again!

57. **Charades.** Split into teams. Make up things for the other people to guess. You can have regular categories like books and movie titles, but categories like animals, shapes, and cartoon characters work well too. Each team takes turns guessing. No talking!

58. **Spies.** Create your own code and send each other secret messages. Take turns hiding a "special object" (really anything weird and non-perishable will do, a wooden

spoon, a tacky gift, a creepy statue) and leaving clues for the other spies to find. The spy who decodes the messages and finds the object, hides the object in a new location with new clues. The hunt begins again.

59. **BINGO.** Ah, the favourite game of gamblers, toddlers, and the elderly! Download and print off some bingo cards or have the kids make their own. Use pennies or buttons for markers or have them colour in the square when it's called. Have one adult randomly select the numbers, words or pictures. You win bingo by collecting a straight line, or of you want to mix things up, win by collecting the corners, an x or z shape, or filling up the entire card.

60. **Nerf war. (Or airplane war)** If you already have Nerf guns, great you're good to go, but if you don't you can create paper airplanes and use these instead. Set the ground rules for areas that are off limits and body parts that can't be hit. Create teams or decide to go solo. Set time limits, hit limits or no limits... and let the fun begin!

61. **Domino run and/or Rube Goldberg machines.** Set up your dominos, or other materials with the intention of creating a pattern or noise when you knock them down. If you get good at this you can even have a simple task for the knocked down dominos to accomplish, like pushing a ball into a cup, or hitting a stick that drops a "trap" onto a stuffed animal. There's lots of examples online, but my favourite to watch is the band OK Go. If you get good at this it can be addicting!

62. **Video game tournament.** Set up your favourite video games. Take turns playing each other and cheering everyone on. If it's a one player game be sure to set a timer or the game will take over!

63. **Create a book.** Fold several pages of blank paper, stapling together on the fold. Divide each page in half, half for a picture, half for the story. Either have your children create the story and pictures entirely on their own, or write down what they dictate. Set a time for when the book will need to be done. Have everyone gather and share their stories, it's sure to be entertaining.

64. **Meal of History!** Have the kids research a historical figure. Using items from around the house each person dresses up as someone from that period of history and comes to dinner. Everyone takes turns guessing, one guess at a time, who has come to dinner. You can reuse this idea with any category you or the kids like and feel free to give out mealtime "prizes" like… the winner doesn't have to clean up their plate, or receives an extra dessert!

65. **Make window decorations and messages for the world outside.** You'll enjoy communicating with the outside world and people who pass your window will enjoy the art. Make sure that the pictures and words are large enough to be seen from the street.

66. **Chore Time Madness.** Give everyone a chore or a list of tasks. Gather everyone in a central location, play some inspiring music, ready the timer and give the signal to START! The first person to finish their chores and do a good job gets a prize! At our house the prize was usually getting first pick of a TV show or games. It was hotly contested! This was also the way we learned that our twin toddlers could harness their destructive power for good. They could strip a bed clean in under a minute! If only they could use their powers to pick up their toys!

67. **Progressive Dinner.** Eat different parts of the meal in different places in the house. Salad in the living room, chicken in the bedroom, dessert in the hall, variety is what makes it an adventure. Just make sure you do it together!

68. **Learn an "old fashioned" skill.** Perhaps there's something you've always wanted to learn or a skill you already have, but haven't had the time to pass on. Sewing, woodworking, making butter, you name it, the internet has a tutorial to help you learn it! Learn beside the kids and let them watch/do small tasks with you. Depending on their age they will either be a big help, or "help" for a few minutes and move on to the next thing, but both of you will feel a sense of accomplishment and will forget that you are isolated for a few minutes, and that's well worth your time and effort.

69. **I Spy.** Little kids can play this one for hours and most adults don't mind playing along, which is saying something. Take turns picking something visible nearby and giving a clue to the guesser. Say "I spy with my little eye, something that is…" Then give a one word clue like green, round, short. The guesser then guesses until they get it right. Then it's their turn!

70. **Models and big crafts.** Have a "long term" craft that everyone can spend a little time on each day. Dig up the knitting kit Aunt Francis gave you last Christmas. Pull out the lego and make that city you've been talking about. Finish that half glued model of the WW2 aircraft you've had since you were twelve. Start something new. Depending on age and interest the kids will come and go from the task, but you'll enjoy putting something together and all of you will talk about the time you put together something that seemed impossible!

71. **Have an "unbirthday."** Put up birthday decorations, make a cake, have the family sneak into each other's rooms, find a favorite item and wrap it as a gift for the "unbirthday" person. Make sure everyone's names are on the cake. Taking turns, sing "happy unbirthday" to each other and give the "unbirthday persons" their gift. Everyone will laugh to see the weird things people chose to wrap up, and you all get cake!

72. **Weird Workout.** Find work out videos from the 80s or a strange tutorial on Youtube. Try to do the workout, but do it together. Laughing and carrying on is encouraged.

73. **Rearrange your house.** Everyone wishes they had a place for _____. Now's your chance to make that happen. Try furniture in a new room. Clean and rearrange your coffee table and bookshelves. Repurpose a room or closet. You don't have to completely make over a space or move everything there permanently. Try not to worry about perfection. The change will be enough to do you good.

74. **Learn a new card/dice game.** There's a reason card and dice games have been around for centuries. They're easy to carry, you can play with one person or a lot of people, and the rules are usually not that complicated. Little guys like Go Fish, while most people enjoy Gin Rummy, King's Corner or Farkle. Have a little patience and you'll be able to get over the initial learning curve and into the fun zone. Careful though, you might get addicted!

75. **Learn a new language as a family.** Pick a word or two and insist that the new word is used in place of the English word for the whole day. If someone messes up and speaks English instead, make them do a funny "punishment" like jumping up and down on one leg for ten seconds, or patting their head while rubbing their tummy.

76. **Make something practical or beautiful for your home.** Choose a new craft or project that you'll enjoy looking at or using during the isolation. A lovely wreath, a planter box, a photo collage, choose what pleases you most! You can do a project together or choose different projects to work on at the same time. Enjoy each others creations!

"Social-Distancing" Things To Do Outdoors

In The Sun

77. **Scavenger hunt.** Bring a bag or a basket for each hunting group and make a list of things that they need to find and bring home, or locations they have to discover on their walk. When you get back from your hunt have everyone reveal what they found. If you wish you can have each team take a picture of themselves at the location or with the item instead. That way they don't have to touch anything at all!

78. **Plant a garden or just a few flowers.** You can use pre-grown plants, seeds from a package, or try to germinate seeds from fruits and vegetables you bought from the store. Have the kids help dig the holes for the seeds and enjoy seeing how much the plants grow each day. Write your observations down, photograph the stages or simply enjoy.

79. **I Spy outdoor version.** As you go on a walk or sit in the backyard let the kids solve a mystery. "I spy with my little eye something that is…." Give one clue ie: red, square, tall, wavy, and then see if anyone else figures it out! The person who guesses correctly gets to be the leader next.

80. **Tree/Plant identification.** Collect leaves (be careful not to pick anything poisonous or allergy inducing!) Look up the the name etc. of the plant you found. Place leaf be-

tween two pieces of wax paper and iron together. The process will help the leaf to lay flat and keep it from drying out. Cut out leaf and paste to the page of a scrap book or put in a photo album along with the information you found.

81. **Play freeze tag.** One person is "it." If you are tagged by the "it" you stand frozen in place until another non-it person touches you. If the "it" freezes every person playing, they win!

82. **Play soccer, kick ball, or hacky sac.** Since these games don't involve throwing, you can adapt them for a relatively small area. Create goals or just see how many times you can hit or pass the ball before you miss.

83. **Play clap ball.** Use a small rubber ball (like the kind you get in those coin machines at the mall) find a windowless wall with a bit of pavement next to it. A garage or side of the house works well. Throw the ball at the wall so that it bounces down onto the pavement and try to catch it. Once you get good at that, pass it back and forth to a partner. See how many times you can clap before you catch it. Throw underhand, overhand, under your leg, with your back turned… so many possibilities!

84. **Bucket brigade.** Fill one bucket all the way to the top and set it at the start line, put an empty bucket with a ruler in it at the finish. Create an obstacle course. Each person tries to get through the course without spilling.

They then dump the water they've saved into the empty bucket at the end of the course. The water is measured, emptied and then it's the next person's turn.The person who spilled the least amount of water is the winner.

85. **Bug collection.** Either catch bugs and put them in a jar with holes poked in the lid or take pictures of them. Try to find out what kind of bug you caught, what it eats, what it does etc. Make notes and draw a picture in a bug journal. Release the bug and watch where it goes.

86. **Outdoor murals.** Make your own sidewalk chalk or buy some, it lasts a long time! Write messages to each other and to the outside world. Draw lovely pictures. Make a path and have the rest of the family follow it. Make a racetrack for mini cars or for your bikes to follow. Make the plan of a little house for dolls to visit. Draw a master-piece and take a picture.

87. **Picnic.** If you already have a table, that's great, but you can also bring out an old table cloth or blanket, set it on the ground and eat your meal outside. Don't stress too much about what you're eating, the meal doesn't have to be fancy, everything tastes better outdoors, and the new location will do you some good.

88. **Blow bubbles.** Use the store bought version or create DIY bubbles using dish soap and glycerine, (or just dish soap in a pinch.) There's many DIY recipes for bubbles and wands out there and some are pretty spectacular.

There's even a diy rope wand that allows you to create person sized bubbles! Little kids tend to like to chase and catch the bubbles most of all, but everyone enjoys watching bubbles float away!

In the Rain

89. **Rivers.** Make little paper boats or use ice cubes, little sticks or leaves. Find a place where the rain is collecting and "running off." Test your "boats" and see how far you can get. Test other run off locations. Be careful to pick places that are out of the way of traffic and other dangers!

90. **Walk in the Rain.** If it's not thundering and lighting, put on your rubber boots, find your umbrella and go for a walk. Splash in puddles. See what the various animals do during the rain. Enjoy the adventure.

91. **Nesting.** If it *is* thundering and lighting use a porch, or if you don't have one, open a door or window in an area is sheltered enough that you won't get too wet. Make a nest of blankets for the kids and you to cuddle. Watch the light show and count the seconds between the lighting and thunder. Guess if the rain is going to come down harder, or if it's on the way out. Smell the air, it smells light and fresh! It's also a great time to drink hot chocolate.

92. **Science Experiments.** Put a couple of buckets or cups outside in the rain. Have the kids guess how much will be in them and if one cup will have more than the other. After the rain is finished, go out and test the your results. If you are interested you can also test the difference between tap water and rain water.

93. **Make a song or a story.** Sing a song to the rhythm of the rain. Will the thunder work with your song? Make up a story about who is making all the thunderclap noise. Are giants bowling? Maybe a cloud is clumsy and keeps dropping dishes. It's interesting to see what the kids will make up!

94. **Turn out the Lights.** Even if the lights don't go out, turn them off and use flashlights to travel around the house. Create a shadow puppet show. You can even shine the flashlight through the window to see how far the beam goes, and what the rain looks like as it passes through the light.

In the Snow

95. **Forts.** Build a snow fort or use your boots to trace out the lines of a fort or house in the snow. Let the kids add their own sections of the fort or house. A kitchen? Battlements? Lounge? Lots of possibilities.

96. **Build a slide.** Even if you have a small area to build in you can make a ramp for the kids to slide down. If you have packing snow, simply pile the snow together and pat it down to make it hard. If you have hard snow, you'll want a shovel to stack it together. Then either pat the snow together, a lot, or use water to mesh the pieces together. If the kids don't have toboggans plastic garbage bags, or trays will work just fine. The more they try the slide, the better the slide will get. Just watch out for obstacles!

97. **Look at the snow flakes.** Being careful not to get the snow flakes too warm, examine the crystals. It's true, no two are the same. You can take photos or draw pictures of the flakes you discover.

98. **Painted snow.** Get a couple of spray bottles, fill with water and add food colouring. The kids can write messages. Paint a snow man or decorate their fort. Be careful with this one though, the kids might choose to decorate each other!

99. **Trek to the Arctic Circle.** Pack a backpack with snacks and a thermos of hot chocolate. Hike through a "wilderness" area. If you don't have access to one it could just be your yard or down your street. Be sure to point out all the "sights" like Polar Bears, Seals and Frozen Explorers. When you are "exhausted" stop and have a snack. Say things like "I sure am glad we packed these provisions." Or "Good thing we didn't have to eat Timmy. That would have been awkward." When you get back inside snuggle everyone in blankets and talk about your adventure.

100. **Glow People.** Since the days are shorter you can have fun during the dark hours by taping glow sticks to your kids snowsuits to create stick people, or make fascinating shapes. It's really fun to take your kids for a walk as a family of stick people and watch the reactions!

101. **Crystal Palace.** Carefully collect icicles using a long pole. Be sure you or the kids aren't standing under the icicle as it falls! Assemble the icicles upright in the snow or add them to your fort. They make a really interesting window. Take photos through the icicle. Shine a flashlight through the icicles and note the way the light goes through the ice.

5

. . . .

Your time together in isolation presents so many challenges, to your health, mental well-being, and your family, but it is more than possible to survive these days and build strong ties with those you love.

Remember, you are of great value to those around you. Your loved ones are travelling through this time with you and will need your help to get through the isolation and out the other side.

Don't forget, you need these people too. They are helping you, in their own way, and "future you" will certainly look back and be able to see all the valuable ways they got you through these days. Of course, you don't have to wait for the future to figure that out, you can learn to see their help in the here and now.

Look for their smiles and encouragement, hear when they say thanks and take it for what it is…thanks! Be with them in the moment. Listen. Respond. Love and be loved. There is so little in life that you truly need, isolation has a way of paring life down to the things that really matter. Take advantage of that lesson.

When children are being difficult, or the tasks in front of you seem impossible, be encouraged, even a small effort can pay off in ways you could never imagine.

You don't have to be Maria, but you can make the best of what you have and manage your situation. You can create a routine. You can have fun, even when your situation seems very dark indeed.

I hope that you will take away the courage to be creative with your situation, and that you will avoid feeling that you must manage everything or that you can't manage anything at all. We all feel that way from time to time. As I am fond of saying to my kids,

"Sure you feel that way, but is it true?"

Feelings are often, just feelings. The truth is another matter. The fact that you picked up this book at all should say to you that you are trying, that you are making a difference, that you'll find a way through this.

Remember, every moment doesn't need to be a success. Plans fail. You'll fail. Forgive and keep trying. It will be ok.

As my mother used to say,
"Take heart. This too shall pass."

Enjoy this book?
Want to try another?

Check out NorthSouth Entertainment's other offerings here:
https://www.northsouthentertainment.com

You can sign up for our mailing list and find out what else Maureen & Laureen have up their sleeves!

https://www.northsouthentertainment.com/contact-us

We'd love to connect with you!

If you loved this book I'd love a review! Each review helps this little book reach more people, and I'd appreciate hearing what worked for you and your family.

About Laureen

Laureen's work has taken her from page to stage, rehearsal room to screen and back again.

She is one half of the dynamic team behind NorthSouth Entertainment, where she works as a writer, composer, director and actor for the screen, stage and musicals. Most recently, she wrote music and lyrics, and directed the readings for the musical, "I Once Was Lost."

Laureen lives with her four lovely children and wonderful husband in Ontario, Canada.

Other Titles By Laureen

"Hope Springs, Hope Clings! Poems for Hope and Love in this World"

"Heart of Gold," the Musical

www.ingramcontent.com/pod-product-compliance
Lightning Source LLC
Chambersburg PA
CBHW020037040426
42331CB00031B/922